Systems of Government

THEOCRACY

Sean Connolly

A+

Smart Apple Media

Published by Smart Apple Media, an imprint of Black Rabbit Books
P. O. Box 3263, Mankato, Minnesota 56002
www.blackrabbitbooks.com

Library of Congress Cataloging-in-Publication Data
Connolly, Sean, 1956-
 Theocracy / Sean Connolly.
     pages cm. -- (Systems of government)
 Summary: "Describes what the theocratic system of government is, how religions play a role in the laws and morals of the citizens. The history of how theocracies have evolved, the rise and fall of religions, and the future of theocratic governments are examined"--Provided by publisher.
 Includes index.
 ISBN 978-1-59920-806-0 (library binding)
 1. Theocracy--Juvenile literature. I. Title.
 JC372.C66 2013
 321'.5--dc23
                          2012000152

Created by Appleseed Editions Ltd,
Designed by Hel James
Edited by Mary-Jane Wilkins
Picture research by Su Alexander

Picture credits
Page 5 AFP/Getty Images; 6 Keystone/Getty Images; 9 Daily News L P (New York)/Getty Images; 10 Stephan Gladieu/Getty Images; 13 &14 Photos.com/Thinkstock; 16 AFP/Getty Images; 18 Getty Images; 21, 22 & 25 AFP/Getty Images; 26 Time & Life Pictures/Getty Images; 28 Shutterstock; 30 Donna Day/Getty Images; 33 Zzvet/Shutterstock; 34 Sylvain Grandadam/Getty Images; 37 Getty Images; 39 ArabianEye/Getty Images; 41 AFP/Getty Images; 42 Photos.com/Thinkstock; 44 Getty Images

Printed in the United States of America at Corporate Graphics, North Mankato, Minnesota.

PO1445
2-2012

9 8 7 6 5 4 3 2 1

Contents

What Is a Theocracy?

One of the greatest human achievements is the way in which communities of all sizes agree on a system of rights and laws that binds them together. People within the community might disagree about the exact nature of the rights and laws—as rival candidates do during an election—but they share an overall belief in the system.

Their trust is usually placed in organizations (such as a parliament or congress) or in individuals (a prime minister, president, or king). Either way, the population agrees that individuals or groups—people like themselves—can shape the way in which they live as a society.

Some societies, however, look beyond their immediate surroundings for guidance on how to live together. If they share a strong religious belief, they might use sacred writings and traditions to guide them in their daily lives. Societies that use religious principles to govern their people are called theocracies. Like the words for some other forms of government (such as **democracy** and autocracy), theocracy is made up of two Greek words. The "cracy" comes from *kratos*, meaning rule or strength. But it is "theo" (from *theo*, meaning God) that defines this system.

Combining Systems

Other systems of government represent the wishes of all the people through their elected representatives (as in a democracy) or follow the rule of a powerful individual (as in a **dictatorship**). A theocracy works differently. It exists because people want to combine their religious beliefs with their political system.

This book examines how and why theocracies come about and how well they work as systems of government. A number of questions surrounding theocracies are discussed including:
• Do people in theocracies believe the system is fair and does the people's view of fairness matter if they look to God for answers?
• Who decides which version of Christianity, **Islam**, **Buddhism**, or **Judaism** should take precedence in the community or country?

• Can elements of theocracy coexist with other forms of government?
• Are there likely to be more or fewer theocracies in the future?

The framework of world politics is rapidly changing. Most likely, today's answer to that last question is different from people's predictions 15 or 50 years ago.

Prince William and Catherine Middleton were married in London in April 2011. If William becomes king, he will also become supreme governor of the Church of England —a centuries-old merging of church and state.

Political Beliefs

From the earliest times, societies have developed different forms of government to impose order and reflect their shared values. Most of those forms of government chose leaders from among themselves or accepted the leadership of a powerful individual. But in the past, many communities (and even some countries) allowed their religious beliefs to guide their political life.

MILESTONES IN THEOCRACY

3100 BC	Upper and Lower Egypt are unified under one ruler who is considered divine, and is served by extensive priesthood
539 BC	Kingdom of Judah operates as a theocracy for six centuries after the return of the Jews from Babylon
ca. AD 70	Jewish historian Flavius Josephus creates the term "theocracy" to distinguish government of the Jews from other types of government
622	Prophet Muhammad establishes Islamic theocracy in Medina
800s–1870	Papal States operate as Catholic theocracy
1260	Kublai Khan converts to Buddhism and approves theocracy in Tibet
1525	Huldrych Zwingli transforms Zurich into a theocratic state
1532–1535	Anabaptist theocracy governs German **city-state** of Münster
1554	John Calvin establishes strict **Protestant** theocracy in Geneva
1616	Buddhist theocracy is established in Bhutan
1630s	English **Puritans** establish theocratic governments in the colonies of Massachusetts and Connecticut
1847	**Mormon** settlers establish short-lived state of Deseret in the American West before Utah becomes a state
1885–1898	Mahdi defeat British forces and establish Islamic theocracy in Sudan
1905	France passes a law guaranteeing separation of church and state
1911–1919	Mongolia is governed by a Buddhist theocracy
1979	Islamic revolutionaries establish theocratic government in Iran
1996–2001	**Taliban** leaders form Islamic theocracy in Afghanistan

Church and State

Many countries go to great lengths to keep their governments free from religious influence. This attitude is expressed in the phrase "separating church (religion) and state (government)." By choosing to live in a theocracy or making another type of government more theocratic, it means having a completely different view of how people and societies should behave.

A scene in rural Tibet in the 1940s. Tibet was a Buddhist theocracy when the Chinese invaded and seized control in the 1950s.

Separating church and state sets clear boundaries between religious-based ideas of right and wrong and the legal rules. Countries that cherish freedom of religion—people's right to worship as they choose—also try to ensure that no set of religious beliefs can change the laws of the land. For example, a religion might allow a man to have two or more wives, but **polygamy** is against the law in most western countries.

RIPE FOR CHANGE?

Fundamentalism is a response to change and may feed theocratic ideals. The term "fundamentalism" comes from the fundamental (or basic) beliefs a group shares. A group that feels threatened in some way highly values the importance of shared beliefs. Many religious fundamentalists feel threatened by the pace of change in the modern world. Whether they are Muslims who insist on traditional clothing, Christians who use the Bible to teach science, or Jewish settlers in the Middle East, fundamentalists look to the past for guidance on how to behave now and in the future.

Fundamentalist views can be very powerful, drawing more people toward them and shaping the direction in which a society—or country—will take in the future.

Being linked to a certain religion may harm a politician's chances in countries with a strong tradition of separating church from state. John F. Kennedy was Catholic and faced strong opposition from many American voters when he ran for president in 1960. Some people feared that because he was Catholic, he would allow the ideas of the pope to influence his decisions as president. Kennedy pointed out that he was running for president not as a Catholic, but as an American, and people should not be judged politically based on their religious beliefs.

Despite politicians' efforts to keep the state free of church influence, observers in the United States and other western countries have noticed how the two elements collide more and more frequently (see Voice of the People). As more Muslim countries turn to their Islamic faith in political matters, theocratic ideas are alive and well in the twenty-first century.

Back to Fundamentals

Today, people are accustomed to hearing the word "fundamentalist" in news stories linked to a particular set of religious beliefs. For example, Islamic fundamentalists might stage a protest in Iraq, or Christian fundamentalists in the UK might disagree with a TV series or a subject being taught in schools.

Strong fundamentalists often have a cast-iron certainty that their beliefs are right and all opposing beliefs are wrong. This hard-line view is an echo of earlier times when people went to war over religious differences. It is also a reaction against what many fundamentalists believe were decades of relaxed attitudes in the modern world. As the pace of change has increased, so has the strength of reaction. Will this conflict lead to more theocracies?

A Christian activist holds a placard and cross outside the Supreme Court in Washington D.C., in March 2000. He is demonstrating his support of prayer in America's public (or state) schools.

VOICE OF THE PEOPLE

CHURCH AND STATE IN AMERICA

Jean Bethke Elshtain is an expert on the role of religious belief in American society. She believes it is wrong to expect American political life to be free from religious influence. Her words might well apply to other western countries in the future: "Separation of church and state is one thing. Separation of religion and politics is something else altogether. Religion and politics flow back and forth in American civil society all the time—always have, always will."

Is a Pure Theocracy Possible?

It may not be possible to find a society that is a pure theocracy. However, the search for an example reveals how often humans have looked beyond themselves for guidance on how to live and be ruled. When we try to identify theocracies, we need to look for societies that have placed their trust in some form of higher being.

This photo of a Mormon family was taken in 2008. The family consists of one husband and three wives (two of whom are not legally married to the husband) plus 21 children. The husband and his wives are unofficially continuing the early Mormon practice of polygamy.

THE STORY OF DESERET

In 1847, members of the Church of Jesus Christ of the Latter-day Saints (Mormons) established a settlement called Deseret in what is now the state of Utah. Few people lived in this semi-desert area, which ensured the Mormons that those elected in Deseret supported Mormon principles. The Mormons wanted Deseret to become an American state, but the US government refused to accept some Mormon customs, including polygamy.

As a Mormon theocracy, Deseret could not become a US **territory** (the first step toward becoming a state). Instead, the government reduced its size and called it the Territory of Utah in 1850. Many Mormons were unhappy and continued to obey the laws of the unofficial government known as the State of Deseret. They continued to press for a state with purely Mormon principles, but more and more non-Mormons arrived in Utah after America's first coast-to-coast railway was completed in 1869.

Over the next two decades, Utah passed laws that took away much of the Mormon church influence. The Mormon church realized it had to **compromise** and banned polygamy in 1890. That removed the last obstacle to statehood, and Utah officially became a state in 1896.

If you study any current or historical system of government, you will find it difficult to describe any system as purely one type of society. Examples include:
- While the democratic government of ancient Athens was democratic in some ways, many people could not vote, including women, children, foreigners, and slaves.
- During the dictatorship in Italy run by Benito Mussolini in the 1930s, people continued to vote democratically in local and regional elections.

- In the British **monarchy**, Parliament and other democratic institutions hold the real political power; the king or queen is just a symbolic leader.

Necessary Compromises?

In each case, what seems to be one type of political system is usually a mixture of two or more. The same holds true with most theocracies—past and present. Some political systems might have had a king or queen; others retained democratic elements. This might dilute the purity of a theocracy, but it might also be necessary to compromise.

Why might people living in a theocracy want their government to be less extreme? To answer that, we can look at the type of society that chooses a theocratic form of government and determine what is needed to retain such a system. A theocracy can only develop when people share religious values and agree about the rules and punishments their beliefs dictate. This type of society might be difficult for those in modern western countries to imagine as most western countries allow a huge range of beliefs (and disbeliefs)—but there have been long periods of history when people have followed a universally shared religion.

The everyday lives of people in ancient Egypt are an example. Their lives revolved around an intricate set of shared beliefs, yet the business of government was run by a strict monarchy in which the pharaoh held great power. In ancient Greece, all Greeks shared traditions associated with their gods, yet the city-states chose either military rule or democracy. The Romans also had a shared religious system, but they chose to live under a republic and then an emperor. In the modern world, only Muslim countries come close to being pure theocracies, but most also have monarchies or a form of representative government.

Generally, experiments with pure theocracy have been brief and undertaken in a relatively small region. The Swiss city of Geneva governed itself as a Protestant theocracy under the leadership of John Calvin in the sixteenth century. Less than a century later, English Puritans created theocracies in New England. In nineteenth-century America, Mormons established a short-lived theocratic government in a place they called Deseret (see page 11).

All of these systems faded. The societies were absorbed into wider, nontheocratic governments. But the beliefs behind these pure theocracies remain alive; many religious people continue to introduce them into modern societies.

MICHAEL SERVETVS HISPA... DE ARAGOVIA

*The Spanish theologian Michael Servetus took the ideas of Martin Luther and John Calvin to new conclusions. Servetus's version of Protestant belief was rejected by Calvin's Geneva, and he was burned as a **heretic** in 1553.*

VOICE OF THE PEOPLE

SILENCING A DISSENTING VOICE

*John Calvin was a religious reformer who left his native France and established a theocracy in Geneva. The penalties for those who **dissented** were harsh and delivered swiftly. The views of the Spanish religious reformer Michael Servetus differed from those of the Geneva theocracy. He was burnt as a heretic on October 27, 1553, on the orders of the Geneva governing council. Calvin describes the execution:*

*"Whoever shall maintain that wrong is done to heretics and blasphemers in punishing them makes himself an **accomplice** in their crime and guilty as they are. There is no question here of man's authority; it is God who speaks, and clear it is what law he will have kept in the church, even to the end of the world. Wherefore does he demand of us a so extreme severity, if not to show us that due honour is not paid him, so long as we set not his service above every human consideration, so that we spare not kin, nor blood of any, and forget all humanity when the matter is to combat for His glory."*

Constitutional Systems

Although few pure theocracies exist in today's world, we should look at how religion sometimes is linked with politics. Church and state might be separate in a country, but how separate are they? Does the **constitution** of a country make special provision for any **denomination**? Theocracy can creep into other forms of government and sometimes in surprising ways.

STATE RELIGIONS

In a number of countries, religious denominations are linked to the government in some way. Although most of these countries also cherish the notion of religious freedom, the church-state link troubles some people. They ask whether it is possible for church and state to relate to each other in a way that does not allow the church to dictate laws (as in an outright theocracy) or allow the government to control the actions of the church.

The government-controlled approach was common in communist countries such as the Soviet Union. There, the government veered between eliminating the Russian Orthodox Church altogether and getting spies to join it so the church would echo government views. Present-day communist countries adopt a similar policy. Cuba is relatively tolerant of Catholicism and other religious beliefs, but it also organizes "religious" groups that support the government.

Currently, state religion generally means one of two things. The first is a religion—usually a Christian denomination—that most citizens in a country follow. These denominations often have the country's name in their titles. Even though many citizens have drifted away from these churches, they are still linked to the country. Some, such as the Church of England, still maintain an official church-state link: the reigning monarch is the head of the Church of England. Others, such as the Church of Sweden, have cut official ties with government, but (on paper at least) they still represent most of the citizens.

Islam is another matter. Many Muslims believe that their faith calls for unity across national boundaries based on shared religion. Although very few Muslim countries can be described as pure theocracies (most have ruling families or representative governments), the religious influence is strong. Its influence can range from national laws to foreign policy (see pages 22–25) through education and the media (see pages 38–41).

French King Henri IV became a Catholic to end the nation's religious wars. He believed that religious rulers should not dictate every aspect of people's lives.

Schoolgirls in traditional Islamic clothing walk to their class in a Swedish secondary school. Some European countries are struggling to absorb immigrant communities with different religious and social customs.

Europe was torn apart by vicious religious conflict through much of the sixteenth and seventeenth centuries. The conflict was between Catholics and Protestants. Four or five centuries ago, religion was far more than a matter of conscience for most. Believers felt that they could save entire populations from eternal damnation by ensuring that people followed the "true faith" (which varied depending on one's viewpoint). Even in this salvation-or-damnation scenario, Europeans began to accept an idea that would reduce bloodshed.

The idea was summed up as "a state follows the religion of its ruler." The phrase underpinned two important treaties: the Peace of Augsburg (1555), which accepted that most of central Europe was religiously divided, and the Peace of Westphalia (1648) that ended the Thirty Years' War. One outcome dramatically changed the balance of power in Europe. After 1648, Catholic Spain no longer claimed political (or religious) control over the Protestant Netherlands.

VOICE OF THE PEOPLE

The Pure Doctrines of Jesus

*The United States was born in the era known as the Age of **Enlightenment**. During this time, new scientific and social ideas linked to widespread education replaced many of the religious certainties of the past. The document that announced the arrival of this new country was the Declaration of Independence and signed on July 4, 1776,—the date of the birth of the United States.*

Thomas Jefferson wrote most of the declaration and later became the third US president. For more than two centuries, his words describe some of the noblest human aims—for equality under the law and the right to "life, liberty and the pursuit of happiness."

Many Americans consider Jefferson as a man who sought to pull the state away from any church. Unlike the country from which America gained its independence, the new nation had no equivalent of the Church of England. But other Americans—hoping that the United States will become a more strongly Christian country—look for clues in some of Jefferson's other writing. In 1816, he wrote: "I have little doubt that the whole country will soon be rallied to the unity of our Creator, and, I hope, to the pure doctrines of Jesus also."

THE VOTING BOOTH

Democracy and Privilege?

Can any government system that allows special privileges to certain religions exist in a country that considers itself to be democratic and representative?

The religious settlements in most European countries date from the turbulent period in the seventeenth century. By the beginning of the eighteenth century, most European countries promised some form of religious freedom even if one denomination was dominant. Countries with state religions, such as Great Britain, allowed other groups freedom of worship.

Laws That Bind

Laws are the heart of any system of government.
Governments create and enforce laws so that society
follows the pattern that its people have chosen. Laws
are an important way of defining a society, whether it is
governed totally or in part through its religious beliefs by
some form of theocracy or whether it professes to keep
church and state separate.

Different Approaches
Countries with a Christian tradition generally avoid preserving the
Christian link in their laws. Laws guaranteeing religious freedom
allow Christians and those who belong to other faiths to worship

VOICE OF THE PEOPLE

SEPARATE OR PLAYING A PART?
In September 2008, Farhan Bhatti, an American Muslim, spoke of the relationship between Islam and US society: "As Muslims, we do indeed believe that Islam is the best system. But we do not live in a Muslim country, nor do we live in a theocracy. When you have Muslims living in a non-Muslim country, Islam does not preclude Muslims from getting involved in the affairs of that country for the betterment of that society. This is, actually, a form of da'wah (an invitation to people to understand Islam) because as more Muslims become involved in society, the misconstrued images and stereotypes that some Americans have in their minds about Muslims will begin to be eradicated."

An Orthodox Jew casts his vote in a polling station in an Israeli election in 2009. Orthodox Jews try to apply the laws and codes of sacred writing in their daily lives.

as they please. A **free press** allows Christian preachers to use the media easily and often (see pages 38–41). At a local level, however, some laws reflect a religious influence. For religious reasons, it was illegal to sell alcohol on Sundays in parts of Wales well into the twentieth century. Similar restrictions still apply in many counties of the United States. Religious believers in these countries can shape laws on a local level.

Many Muslims believe that their religion calls for a single, Islamic state that would include all people of that faith. Such a wide-ranging state, called the caliphate, would wipe away many of the national boundaries that currently exist. The set of laws known as **sharia** (see page 24) is at the heart of the Islamic religion. Presently, that goal is still an ideal, and Muslims must maintain their beliefs either in a country with a majority-Muslim population (such as Egypt or Indonesia) or as a **minority** in a more diverse society (such as the UK, United States, or Australia).

Widespread discussion in many countries regarding religious laws —and how they relate to the wider country—has led to some surprises. Many British people, for example, fear that any introduction of sharia would threaten the Christian traditions of the country. However, Rowan Williams, Archbishop of Canterbury (and the highest-ranking Anglican **cleric**), has stated that the introduction of some aspects of sharia is "unavoidable." Otherwise, many British Muslims would find it difficult to relate to the British legal system.

FRANCE'S BAN ON THE BURKA

France has a tradition of religious freedom as do many western countries. Its national motto, "Liberty, equality and brotherhood," dates to the time of the French **Revolution** in 1789. Before the revolution, the political system ensured that the Catholic Church had special privileges. When those privileges were abandoned after 1789, the French were proud to promote and support religious freedom. A 1905 law calls for French society to be **secular** and that religious clothing cannot be worn in schools or public places.

But a dispute over one item of clothing caused the French to reexamine the boundaries between church and state. The dispute spills over into questions of terrorism, racism, and the role of women. The piece of clothing is the burka, an enveloping outer garment that covers nearly all of a woman's body and sometimes her face.

France has one of the largest Muslim minorities (about 7 percent) in western Europe. Ever since a bitter civil war in Algeria (a Muslim country and former French colony) in the 1990s, the relationship between non-Muslim French people and the immigrant Muslim community has been strained. With the rise of **Islamist** terrorism in other parts of the world, tensions became more acute.

French politicians have tried to find a balance between maintaining the secular tradition (some see the burka as a religious symbol) and the wider issue of religious freedom. In 2003, the French government banned women's headscarves (common in the Muslim community) because they were considered religious symbols. Seven years later, it passed a law forbidding people to conceal their faces in public places. This law was partly an antiterrorist measure. Police and security forces need to identify people's faces, but many Muslims viewed it as targeting women in their community.

A French Muslim woman in full burka is accompanied by a supporter as she makes a symbolic protest outside the French National Assembly in Paris.

THE VOTING BOOTH

Symbols of Faith

Do you think that the French ban of the burka is a justified way of keeping French society free from religious influence? Is it an attack on religious freedom? What about a Christian cross or a Jewish star of David?

Islamic Crossroads

Jewish and Christian societies have lived under theocracies briefly during the course of their long histories, but theocracy as a system of government has never taken root permanently. By and large, Jews and Christians accept that their religious and national responsibilities do not overlap. Muslims face different pressures. Many are happy to follow the Jewish and Christian examples of separating church and state on a personal level. Others believe that being a Muslim is the most important thing and that the Islamic faith should underpin everything.

Fundamental Differences

Many Christians and Jews strongly feel that their religious beliefs should be the foundation of their countries' laws. But they also see that this goal is probably unrealistic. Instead, they approach secular government in one of two ways. Some groups, such as Amish Christians and Hasidic Jews, remove themselves from society as much as possible or impose strict rules about clothing and behavior. Others, prompted by television preachers (see pages 38–41) and other believers, hope to introduce their ideas into politics, education, and society in general.

Those two approaches allow believers to stay true to their faith while accepting others around them who do not share their faith. They also follow an instruction that Jesus gave: "Render unto Caesar the things that are Caesar's and unto God the things that are God's." Most people agree that Jesus told his followers that they could obey the rules of a government (even if it is led by nonbelievers) as long as they were true to their faith on a personal level.

Some Muslims take a different view. They believe in striving for entirely Muslim societies in which Islam guides every aspect of people's lives as well as all of society's laws and international behavior. They look back to the period immediately after the death of Muhammad, the founder of Islam, in the seventh century. At that time, Muslims tried to ensure that the moral and legal heart of Islam would survive under the caliphs (successors) of Muhammad.

Islam spread widely across Asia and north Africa and into Europe during the seventh and eighth centuries. Country boundaries (for example, between Algeria and Morocco or Iraq and Iran) mattered very little to Muslims. At that time, the people living within the wider Muslim area —known as the caliphate—believed that sharia (Islamic law—see panel) should apply equally and everywhere.

Finding it difficult to build and maintain this unified Islamic nation, the Muslims lived in other kingdoms and countries with national boundaries. But the goal of building a huge, united Muslim nation— a new caliphate—still exists for many Muslims. Political specialists use

Supporters of the Muslim Brotherhood, an officially banned political movement that wants to implement Islamic law in Egypt, stage a protest about the conduct of Egypt's elections in 2005. The Brotherhood, no longer banned, may likely gain influence in the future.

SHARIA LAW

Islamic law holds Muslim communities together and underpins the ideas of a caliphate. This code of laws is known as sharia, which is an Arabic word that means the well-worn path to water. The roots of Islam are in the Arabian Desert, so a path to water is a powerful symbol of the Muslim quest for truth and justice. They believe that Islam provides that "water" as long as people follow its guidance.

Sharia is a mixture of statements from the Koran (Islam's sacred writing) and the writings of Islamic scholars over the past 15 centuries. Governments that have introduced the most theocratic elements in recent years—Iran, Saudi Arabia, and Afghanistan, for example—have based their systems of politics, justice, and doing business on sharia.

In some instances, the outside world views sharia justice as primitive and even barbaric. Punishments in some countries include cutting hands off or stoning people to death. Taken as a whole, sharia offers believers a merciful way of living together. Religious leaders from other faiths have recognized this special role of sharia. Dr. Rowan Williams, Archbishop of Canterbury and the most senior figure in the Church of England, points out that sharia is often misunderstood by outsiders and that it has a long tradition of inspiring Muslims as well as people beyond the Islamic community.

An Indonesian sharia official canes a woman as a punishment for having a relationship with a man who was not her husband. Many non-Muslims find such punishments barbaric.

the word Islamism to describe this form of political Islam, and Islamist is used to describe someone who promotes it. Islamism lies at the heart of many disputes within and between Muslim countries; some terrorists even use it to justify violence against non-Muslims.

The widespread protests in many Muslim countries through 2011—known collectively as the Arab Spring—have highlighted the issue of Islamism. Protesters joyfully overthrew dictators and pressed for greater democracy. In several of those countries, though, the most powerful political groups hold Islamist views and may have great influence after elections are held.

VOICE OF THE PEOPLE

Fear and Sadness

The Taliban are a group of Islamists who held power in Afghanistan during the 1990s and hope to regain that control. They followed a chilling interpretation of sharia law with public executions and strict control of the people (especially women). Some fear that the democratic uprisings of the Arab Spring could encourage more such brutal governments.

The following comment on Reuters news agency website, days after Colonel Gaddafi's capture and execution in Libya, typifies those fears: "This is all very sad. Everything about the uprising and the government's attempts to stop it. Before the uprising, Gaddafi was a moderate leader as far as Arab leaders go. Should we be concerned that the uprisings (Arab Spring) will bring in radicals who will align with other radicals as they pursue a **totalitarian** way of life? Yes. Already, the Christians in Egypt have suffered great death and deprivation at the hands of the freedom fighters. A goal of the radicals is to unite the Arab world under one caliphate and restore a global Muslim rule. I am concerned."

A Lasting Legacy

A government does more than make rules and regulations for its people. It builds ways of thinking, which linger—sometimes as dim memories, sometimes in people's attitudes—well beyond the lifetime of that government. Whole nations, it seems, retain memories in the same way that individuals do.

"A PEOPLE OF GOD"

Cotton Mather was a Puritan minister and author who lived in Massachusetts during the seventeenth and eighteenth centuries. In 1692, he wrote about the special nature of his fellow New Englanders: "The New Englanders are a People of God settled in those which were once the Devil's Territories, and it may easily be supposed that the Devil was exceedingly disturbed when he perceived such a People here accomplishing the Promise of old made unto our Blessed Jesus, That he should have the Utmost parts of the Earth for his possession."

Roger Williams, the Baptist preacher and founder of Rhode Island, is one of the international figures honored by the Reformation Monument in Geneva, Switzerland.

English citizens, for example, retained enough good memories of monarchy to welcome Charles II to rule 21 years after his father, King Charles I, was executed in the English Civil War. The French did not lose their taste for independence and democracy while their country was controlled by the Germans during the World War II. Some political observers look at the harsh laws in modern Russia and conclude that Russian people expect strictness after centuries of absolute monarchy and then **communism**.

Echoes of the Past

Theocracy has a similar effect on people's views. Elements of life under a theocracy remain long after the system of government has been abandoned by a community. These could be called folk memories that are recalled in unlikely forms. In Massachusetts, for example, diners can stop for lunch at the Pilgrim Café. They might wear Puritan brand sports shirts or Mayflower brand tennis shoes. All of these names refer to the seventeenth century when the first English settlers (the Pilgrims) arrived on the *Mayflower* ship. These settlers formed a theocracy guided by strict Protestant (Puritan) beliefs.

The company names are reminders of the past and have no real connection to the modern world. Or do they? Until 2004, more than three centuries after the Puritan theocracy ended, people in Massachusetts could not buy alcoholic drinks on a Sunday. The Sunday ban still applies in neighboring Connecticut. The "no alcohol sales on Sunday" laws in these states reflect the opinion of seventeenth-century lawmakers when both states were theocracies.

Outdated regulations dating from stricter religious periods are known as blue laws. These may seem absurd to modern people (see panel right), but the laws remain even if they have not been enforced for, many years.

People who have no religious beliefs may argue in favor of such laws. One example is the debate about Sunday trading (buying and selling) in the UK. Until recently, the only shops that were permitted to open on Sundays were small convienience stores and newspaper and magazine shops. Like the New England blue laws, the restrictions dated back to a time when religious thinking lay behind the laws. Many people argued that Sundays might be the only day when workers could shop if they worked on other days. Gradually, the British government allowed more freedom for many types of shops to open. Some of the strongest opposition came from trades unions. They argued that keeping Sundays special guaranteed that workers would have a chance to rest after a busy working week.

Even if people pay little attention to blue laws and other relics of a more religious past, their attitudes may reflect the values that led to those laws. The United States is a good example. Compared with similar countries in the western world, the American government offers few automatic benefits to its citizens. Americans pay for their medical care and receive far less government support when they are out of work.

Most Americans believe that their system is normal and that Europeans expect more support from their governments. One major reason for this difference in attitudes can be traced to America's religious history. Its most influential European settlers in the seventeenth century, the English Puritans, valued self-reliance and hard work. These values linger in the United States. Most people believe these values are responsible for their actions and expect far less outside help if things go wrong.

Americans in many states have to hide open bottles of alcohol inside brown paper bags if they want to drink in public. This is a legacy of the antialcohol attitudes of the seventeenth-century Puritans.

BLUE LAWS

Rules and regulations that once echoed strongly held religious views, but no longer apply to the modern world, are called blue laws. Most of these remain unchanged but are ignored among the other laws of a county, state, or country. Why? Governments fear that if they begin to get rid of dozens of laws because they are outdated or ridiculous, people might question whether other laws could be safely ignored.

Some of the most absurd examples of blue laws that still exist (even though they are not enforced) include:

- It is illegal to wear a false moustache if it causes laughter in a church (Alabama).
- A man may not kiss his wife on a Sunday (Hartford, Connecticut).
- It is illegal to walk a cow down Main Street after one p.m. on a Sunday (Little Rock, Arkansas).
- Households will be fined if they keep Christmas decorations up after January 14 (Maine).
- It is illegal to eat peanuts in church (Massachusetts).
- A husband may beat his wife as long as he does so in public, on a Sunday, and on the courthouse steps (Huntington, West Virginia).
- It is an offense to hang clothes out to dry on a Sunday (Switzerland).

Are Blue Laws a Bad Thing?

Which of the following views do you agree with?

YES: They're ridiculous and have no place in the modern world.

NO: They're harmless and once people realize some (unenforced) laws are silly, they might lose respect for other laws.

In God We Trust?

A society of religious believers might think it would be easy to base a government on religious principles. But it is not a clear-cut solution. Will the government be Christian? If so, which of the thousands of Christian denominations should rule? Or will the government be Jewish? If so, which Jewish traditions of religious practice would be followed? Many Jews consider themselves to be part of an ethnic group rather than a denomination. Muslims follow traditions such as Shi'a or Sunni, both of which share the same fundamental Islamic beliefs. However, their political differences cause hostility.

THE PLEDGE OF ALLEGIANCE

"I pledge **allegiance** to the flag of the United States of America, and to the republic for which it stands, one nation under God, indivisible, with liberty and justice for all."

Since 1892, Americans have recited the Pledge of Allegiance as a mark of loyalty to their country (with the flag as its symbol). However, at the start of the Cold War in the late 1940s, many Americans wanted to contrast their country with their enemy—the Soviet Union, which was atheist under communism. This is why the words "under God" were added to the American pledge in 1954. Those two words have divided Americans. Many feel these words capture national opinion. Others believe that their country should not have an established (state) religion.

A group of young American children pledge allegiance to the US flag at the start of every school day. How many of them are aware of the dispute surrounding the words "under God," which they will recite?

Deep Rifts

Disputes and lingering disagreements are a part of most religions. Christianity was more or less united for the first few centuries of its existence, but it is difficult to calculate precisely how many separate denominations describe themselves as Christian. Jews also divided themselves into categories (liberal, orthodox, reform) depending on their interpretation of Biblical laws.

Even Islam, the faith that has come closest to producing lasting theocracy, has its share of sharp divisions. Muslims look back to a time when, led by the Prophet Muhammad, they agreed how to put the words of the Koran into practice. The principal division within Islam is between its Shi'a and Sunni branches and goes back to the years following Muhammad's death. Disputes arose about who should be the prophet's rightful successor and which form of religious practice should govern Islam. Today's news reports about terrorist attacks and suicide bombers can be traced back to the same Shi'a-Sunni split.

The Shi'a-Sunni rift is a huge obstacle to forming a single, united Islamic country or caliphate. Which tradition would Islamic judges follow in deciding on divorces, robbery, or murder? Would members of the other tradition abide by such decisions? Similar splits and religious rivalries spelled the end of Christian theocracies in fifteenth-century Florence (with its Catholic theocracy), sixteenth-century Geneva (Calvinist Protestant), and seventeenth-century Massachusetts (Puritan Protestant).

Fearing Theocracy

Another source of unease is the relationship between religious and secular forces in many countries. Countries with clear guidelines about separating church and state often have large numbers of religious believers within their borders. Conflict arises when secularists fear that religious beliefs are gaining too much influence. These fears can be reversed when believers accuse "godless" people of restricting their religious freedom.

India, the world's second-largest country in terms of population, has experienced some of the most violent religious disputes. It is the largest country in what was once a colony known as British India. When Britain granted the colony independence in 1947, it divided the region along religious lines. Many faiths are represented in the area, but the main religions are Hindu and Muslim.

Hindus and Muslims lived together under British rule, but problems arose as the British prepared to grant independence to the region. Hindus made up the majority in much of the Indian peninsula, and Muslims were the larger group to the east and west. The British divided India into the country known as India (the Hindu center) and the Muslim-dominated Pakistan to the east and west. East Pakistan became known as Bangladesh in the 1970s.

Modern India's population may be mainly Hindu, but its constitution grants freedom to Muslims, Christians, and members of other faiths. Some fundamentalist Hindus, however, object to the presence of these "foreign" faiths. Violence has erupted in areas where these religious groups live near each other.

The United States seems to have clear guidelines. On one hand, it has a constitution that prohibits any form of state religion. On the other, it has one of the highest church-going populations in the industrialized world. At times, the two forces seem to be on a collision course.

THE VOTING BOOTH

The National Day of Prayer

Since 1952, US presidents have issued a proclamation that a designated day (usually the first Thursday in May) should be a National Day of Prayer. The idea seems harmless, and President Obama has carried on the tradition. But opponents say that setting aside a day for the purpose of praying is introducing theocracy into what should be a secular society. They refer to the First Amendment to the US Constitution, which states: "Congress shall make no law respecting an establishment of a religion, or prohibiting the free exercise thereof."

Do you think that a national day of prayer establishes a religion, or do you feel that the protests are going too far?

A Hindu monk offers up a prayer on the banks of the River Ganges, which is sacred to India's Hindus. Some members of the Hindu community go beyond traditional ceremonies and attack their non-Hindu neighbors.

End of the Line

Theocracies tend to fade into more common forms of government such as monarchy, democracy, or even dictatorship. Some of the reasons for this are usually apparent from the start. Even in a society that shares most fundamental beliefs, disagreements can threaten a theocratic government. It is difficult for people to agree on the right religious formula to transform politics and even more difficult to stay true to a formula when the government faces a range of nonreligious problems every day.

Politics as Usual?

It is easy to concentrate on the religious nature of theocracies. Citizens of those countries and observers on the outside can identify many of the elements that relate to religious rule—the harsh punishments, the control of the media (see pages 38–41), and the

LEAVING THE AMISH
Saloma Furlong is the author of Why I Left the Amish, *an account of her childhood in a strict Amish community in Ohio. Most Amish people are descendants of Protestants from Germany and Switzerland who fled to America in the eighteenth century to avoid religious persecution. They believe that much of the modern world is corrupt and that they can only be true Christians by keeping themselves separate from American society as much as possible.*

*Within their separate communities, the Amish live according to religious and social (almost political) customs. Much social and political Amish life centers on working together as a community. If one family loses a barn in a fire, the rest of the community joins together to build a new one. Saloma Furlong found this side of Amish life hardest to leave. She explains her mixed feelings: "If the Amish way of life could be separated from the religion, I may still be living their lifestyle. But I found the religion to be a **punitive** one that embraces the pain of life more than it does the joy of life. Perhaps this is left over from the days when our ancestors endured persecution for their religious beliefs. The way this plays out in the religion is that there is more focus on wrongdoers than on the people who are upstanding members of the community."*

Members of an Amish community in Pennsylvania make their way to a church service. The Amish try to avoid contact with most aspects of the modern world such as electricity and cars.

sober atmosphere. But political experts remind us that theocracies are forms of government and should really be seen as the result of extreme political activity.

The most extreme political activity is a revolution—the violent overthrow of one type of government by supporters of another system. The French Revolution violently replaced a monarchy with a republic; the Russian Revolution replaced a monarchy with a communist system. The government of modern Iran, which many people describe as a theocracy, arose out of the 1979 Islamic Revolution that overthrew the Iranian monarchy.

Revolutions, however, often lose some of their extremism after the initial period of violent change. French revolutionaries, once in power, turned on each other as they tried to be more revolutionary than each other.

Eventually, they compromised by allowing a military leader (Napoleon Bonaparte) to take power. Some modern observers look for signs that Islamic revolutionaries are willing to compromise in Iran.

Surviving Evidence

Many people are not aware that some of the societies most famous for being theocracies once had other types of government with strong religious influences. At the time of John Calvin, sixteenth-century Geneva (see page 13) had strict laws governing church attendance. The intent was to keep Sunday sacred and restrict what people could say or do in public. But the people who made and enforced these laws were not Protestant ministers; they were officials elected in the same way as representatives of Geneva's government had been declared for decades. These officials were heavily influenced by Calvin and his followers, but the mechanics of government remained the same.

The mechanics of government survived Calvin although his influence has not vanished from Geneva. Compared with areas of Switzerland that remained Catholic throughout the sixteenth century, Geneva retains a serious, sober atmosphere. If the strong (some say theocratic) Islamic influence on Iran and Saudi Arabia were to fade in the future, it is likely that the surviving republic (Iran) and monarchy (Saudi Arabia) would include examples of Islamic thinking.

Faith Communities

Other large groups that run along theocratic lines, but are not really governments, pose different problems. Such faith-based communities include many religious groups that set themselves apart from wider society. These distinctions can take the form of:
• distinctive clothing (for example, Hasidic Jews, Rastafarians, and the Amish),
• language (the Amish),
• rules about food and drink (Mormons), and
• medicine (Christian Scientists).

In these communities, the mix of religion and politics is weighted toward religion so the followers are less concerned with taxation, foreign policy, roads, and most of the practical matters that occupy much of a government's time and energy. In their own way, however, these groups can influence their members as strongly as other types of government.

WHEN IT ALL GOES WRONG

Faith communities, when run like theocracies, can sometimes descend into chaos. One extreme example was the end of Jonestown in 1978. During the mid-1950s, a young man named Jim Jones founded the Peoples Temple Christian Church Full Gospel in Indiana. The Peoples Temple aimed to promote racial and social equality. Jones moved Peoples Temple to California in the 1960s, continuing to attract people of all races and helping the local poor and homeless. By the 1970s, Jones was convinced that the US government and other organizations were targeting Peoples Temple. Suspicious of those around him, he accused some of being traitors to the Peoples Temple. Meanwhile, he continued to preach a mixture of Christianity and socialism.

By 1977, newspapers were investigating claims that Jones and Peoples Temple operated as a cult that forced members to do many things against their will and in fear of their lives. Jones and hundreds of his followers fled to a community they had built (Jonestown) in the rainforest of Guyana in South America. The media stories continued. On November 14, 1978, an investigating group from the US Congress, led by Congressman Leo Ryan, flew to Guyana. Threatened by a member of the temple, Ryan chose to return his group to the United States. While boarding the plane, Jones's guards killed Ryan and four members of his group. On November 18, 1978, Jones assembled members of his community by a public hall. The people lined up to drink a purple mixture that contained deadly poison; within minutes, more than 900 people died. Jones died of a self-inflicted gunshot.

American actor Powers Boothe portrayed Jim Jones in a TV movie that reenacted the terrifying events in Jonestown, Guyana, in November 1978.

The Media and Theocracy

Rebels surround a capital city with the aim of overthrowing an unpopular dictator. Government forces with more weapons and ammunition are backed up by patrol helicopters with searchlights and fast-moving troop carriers. The odds against rebel success are poor, but rebels feel they have one weapon that could be decisive—public opinion. If they can let people know that the dictator's end might be in sight, their forces would swell. The question is: how can they get their message to the people?

Many countries have experienced these events. Rebels often have succeeded in using public opinion to turn the tables on a hated ruler. The rebels first step in achieving success is often capturing a radio or television broadcasting center. Rebels might announce victory without having fired a shot, knowing that people will come and help them round up security forces and other hated symbols of an oppressive regime.

Knowledge Is Power

Similar scenes have played out many times with small armed groups achieving their aims because they were able to control the flow of information. Still, unpopular governments remain in power by using **propaganda**, which attempts to convince people that the government is legitimate or that it is powerful enough to crush any opposition. Propaganda played a part during the communist era in Europe when communist governments frequently broadcast images of their fighting forces and weapons.

Why discuss rebel groups and dictators when studying theocracy? The answer is contained in a simple sentence that has been repeated for centuries: Knowledge is power. A dictator can spread information (or knowledge) as propaganda. A rebel group can use it to spark an uprising. The flow of information plays an important role in the area where religion and politics mix.

A man relaxes by watching golf on TV in Dubai. Some people fear that Dubai, and some of its Middle East neighbors, might bow to religious pressure over what they should broadcast.

The word "media" describes a wide range of methods of communication that spread ideas. Nowadays, the media includes not only the written word (books, newspapers, and magazines) but also radio, television, cell phones, and the Internet. Most people agree that the free flow of information provides one of the best defenses of democracy. People can access all sides of an argument to make their decisions.

No one seriously believes that the UK, United States, Australia, or any other country with a free press is likely to become a theocracy. But the freedom these countries enjoy—especially the unregulated freedom of access offered by the Internet—allows people with strongly held religious views to transmit their messages. These people want to shape national laws to reflect their religious views. The most extreme examples are America's televangelists (see panel on next page). This falls short of true theocracy, but a political system could be nudged in a

TELEVANGELISTS AND POLITICS

A government often uses the media to further its own ends. In some Islamic countries, such as Iran and Saudi Arabia (both of which are very theocratic), close control of the media ensures that the approved religious message gets through. Non-theocratic countries, also have a tradition of religious broadcasting. In recent years, many religious broadcasters have tried to influence elections and the way in which countries are governed.

The most extreme examples are in the United States, which has a tradition of huge crowds gathering to hear preachers (mostly Protestant). An evangelist is someone who spreads the gospel. Many evangelists understand the potential of television to spread their message beyond the thousands they might address in a crowd to the millions who watch TV. Some televangelists express strong opinions about the political issues that are debated during campaigning for national elections. Critics see them as upsetting the delicate balance between church and state, but supporters see no problem with this.

particular direction by influences such as the Internet, which is crowded with people eager to mix religion and politics.

Controlling the Flow

How is the flow of information controlled in a theocracy? Can a government really try to stop the flow of ideas? The answer is yes, but the position is changing. All forms of strong government, whether they are dictatorships, communist regimes, or religious-influenced systems, want to promote the appearance of unity in their country.

When most of a country's people hold similar core beliefs, it is easier for a theocratic government to control what people can and should be able to read or watch? After all, who would want to face the charge that they were promoting evil religious views in what they wanted to read, write, or watch? A theocracy, like any other form of government, must meet the basic needs of its people for food, shelter, education, and housing. It can expect protests if it fails to do so. If a theocratic government is accused of manipulating information, it may respond that it is only trying to protect the people from bad ways of thinking.

Leading Protestant preacher Eddie Villanueva has been a presidential candidate in the Philippines twice. His huge political rallies resemble enthusiastic religious meetings.

THE VOTING BOOTH

Control What People See and Hear?

In countries that cherish freedom of worship, what sort of limits should be placed on the spread of religious ideas? Should there be complete freedom? Should religion be kept in a church or temple as opposed to the television and newspapers? Is a compromise possible between informing the public about religion and forcing religious views on them?

Looking Ahead

Predicting the future, in the area of international politics, is very tricky. It is easy to draw inaccurate conclusions from recent evidence. Some trends seem to go in one direction then veer in another for unexpected reasons. Hidden currents of public opinion may go unnoticed by political experts for some time and then suddenly burst on the scene.

One expert prediction made by the founders of communism, Karl Marx and Friedrich Engels, turned out to be wrong. Both believed that the first communist governments would be formed in Britain and Germany in the late nineteenth century due to their highly developed factories. Instead, communism first took root in one of the world's least industrialized countries, Russia.

Similarly, most political experts today did not forsee the growing sense of dissatisfaction of people in the Middle East, most of whom live in some of the most strictly controlled countries in the world. Yet, a wave of protests swept leaders from power and threatened others across north Africa and the Middle East in what has become known as the Arab Spring (see page 45).

The Way of the Future?

What place does theocracy have in predictions for the twenty-first century? Most people believe that the age of theocracies is over, and the stage is set for more democracies, dictatorships, and perhaps even modified monarchies. That dismissal of theocracy may be wrong for a number of reasons.

It is possible that some forms of theocracy might thrive in the future. There is evidence for this based on religious basics—fundamentalism. We know "back to basics" fundamentalism gains ground when people feel threatened by the pace of change. Many people across the world feel such a threat now with issues such as terrorism, economic hardships, and environmental problems.

This reaction to sudden changes is nothing new. The pace of change with new forms of communication can be overwhelming; many fear that greedy people will benefit at the expense of the deserving. Many young people have organized protests to help promote fairer societies along with a more sensible use of the world's resources, including oil. This involvement is sometimes considered left-wing politics because the people want their governments to play a bigger part in solving major problems. But the same modern problems that lead some people to left-wing protests send others to the core of their religious faith.

This image depicts young women working in crowded conditions in a London match factory in 1871. Britain's hundreds of factories led Karl Marx and Friedrich Engels to predict that the first communist revolution would take place in Britain or in equally industrial Germany.

The slogan on the Occupy London banner in late 2011 shows how religion has once again crept into the world of politics. Protesters originally intended to camp in the heart of London's financial center. Instead, they found space (and some support) just outside St. Paul's Cathedral.

Many young people—Christians, Muslims, Jews, Hindus, and Buddhists—are turning to strict interpretations of their faiths as a way of finding certainty in an uncertain world. This religious change also has produced change in the world of politics. Some Muslim countries are considering following Iran's example and allowing their religious leaders to influence the process of making laws. Christian preachers in the United States and across the western world continue to urge their followers to support certain political causes and candidates. Religious values are a powerful force in many countries today.

Religious views seem to be making a comeback as part of the wave of "Occupy" protests that sprang up in cities around the world in late 2011. Tent cities appeared in public squares and plazas; many were near financial centers such as Wall Street in New York and the City of London. The protesters represented a broad range of views. Not all agreed on what to do, but they believed that the international financial system was at fault.

More Theocracy?

The 2011 pro-democracy uprisings in many Muslim countries —including Tunisia, Libya, Egypt, Syria, and Bahrain—have become known as the Arab Spring for two reasons. First, these protests began early in the year (during the spring). The second—the more important—reason is that the protesters called for an end to strict repression in favor of more social freedom. The protests were compared to seedlings in the spring that would soon blossom (into democracy).

Some observers feared that the protests might simply replace one dictatorship with another, religious-based dictatorship. They looked back at the 1979 revolution in Iran, which swept an unpopular leader (the shah) from power but replaced him with a strict Islamic theocracy. In October 2011, just 10 months after Hosni Mubarak was swept from power in Egypt, Muslims and Coptic Christians clashed in bitter riots, leaving 28 Copts dead. Many Egyptian Christians fear for their future if Islamic political parties gain overall power.

Do you think that such fears are understandable in Egypt and throughout the countries of the Arab Spring? Do you think people of all faiths will feel a part of these new societies?

Ten or twenty years earlier, such protests were linked by left-wing protests; the slogans on posters were about jobs, workers, and money. Those themes were on display in 2011 as well. But at least one banner in the Occupy London camp by St. Paul's Cathedral in the City of London had a different message: "What would Jesus do?"

Glossary

accomplice   Someone who helps plan or perform a criminal act and must be punished for it.

allegiance   Loyalty and devotion (to something or to an ideal).

Buddhism   A world religion that developed in India about 2,500 years ago.

city-state   A city and the surrounding area that makes its own laws, much as a country does.

cleric   A person with special training who has responsibilities and an official role within an organized religion.

communism   A political system in which all property is owned by the community. A communist government provides work, health care, education, and housing, but may deny people certain freedoms.

compromise   An agreement between two groups that involves each side giving in a little in order to find common ground.

constitution   A written document that spells out the aims and basic principles of an organization, a political group, or a country.

da'wah   Preaching Islam and especially helping non-Muslims understand more about the religion.

democracy   A form of government in which all, or most of the people, have a say in choosing their leaders.

denomination   A branch of a larger religion; members of a denomination share common traditions.

dictatorship   A form of government in which a single person has complete control and absolute power.

dissent   Political opposition to a government's policies.

Enlightenment   Also known as the Age of Enlightenment, a period during the eighteenth century when European thinkers tried to change society through advances in science and learning.

free press   Media (such as newspapers, magazines, television, and radio) that are free from government control.

fundamentalism   A belief in going back to the basic, core values (the fundamentals) of a religion—especially in response to the modern world.

heretic   Someone who proposes beliefs that are different from a religious group's established set of beliefs.

Islam   A world religion that developed in Arabia in the seventh century; its members, Muslims, believe that its founder, the Prophet Muhammad, received the word of God directly and wrote it in the sacred Koran.

Islamist   Someone who believes that Islam is a religion and a set of political beliefs.

Judaism   A world religion developed among ancient Hebrews that is characterized by a belief in one God with Abraham and Moses as his prophets.

minority   A group that makes up less than half of a larger group.

monarchy   A system of government in which the leader, or national symbol, remains in power for life and is replaced by the rulers of succession.

Mormon   A member of the Church of Jesus Christ of Latter-day Saints and believes in the Christian Bible as well as the Book of Mormon.

polygamy   Having more than one wife or husband.

propaganda   The spreading of news, rumor, and sometimes lies to gain political support or to hurt the reputation of the opposition.

Protestant   A Christian movement that opposed the power of the Catholic church in the sixteenth century.

punitive   Intended as a harsh punishment.

Puritan   A member of a Protestant movement in the sixteenth and seventeenth centuries that wanted to rid (purify) the Church of England of practices that were not mentioned in the Bible.

revolution   Forcibly overthrowing a government and replacing it with another.

secular   Separate from or having nothing to do with religion.

sharia   A set of codes and laws that guides the moral and religious behavior of Muslims.

Taliban   An Islamist group that ruled much of Afghanistan in the late 1990s and is trying to regain power.

territory (in American history)   A region of North America settled by people who wanted it to become part of the United States; a territory needs to meet several requirements before it can be admitted to the United States as a state.

totalitarian   Describes a political system in which the government accepts no limits to its powers and tries to control every aspect of its people's lives.

Books

Connolly, Sean. *Religious Freedom (Campaigns for Change).* Smart Apple Media, 2005.
Lucerne, Same. *Theocracies (Exploring World Governments).* ABDO Pub. Co., 2011.
Woolf, Alex. *Fundamentalism (Ideas of the Modern World).* Raintree, 2004

Websites

Religions of the World
http://www.42explore2.com/religion.htm

The Top Dozen Religions of the World
http://www.godweb.org/religionsofworld.htm

Theocracy
http://www.absoluteastronomy.com/topics/Theocracy

Index